My Favorite REPERTOIRE ALBUM

CONCERT SOLOS FOR THE PIANO

Revised and Edited by

MAXWELL ECKSTEIN

CARL FISCHER, Inc.
62 COOPER SQUARE, NEW YORK 10003
BOSTON • CHICAGO • LOS ANGELES • SAN FRANCISCO

Copyright MCMXLVIII by Carl Fischer, Inc., New York
International Copyright Secured
All rights reserved including public performance for profit.
Printed in U.S.A.

INDEX by COMPOSERS

Albeniz	Seguidilla	42
Brahms	Rhapsodie (Eb Major) Op. 119, No. 4	3
Chopin	Berceuse Op. 57	58
	Étude (Butterfly) Op. 25, No. 9	78
	Étude (Revolutionary) Op. 10, No. 12	114
	Fantaisie-Impromptu Op. 66	98
Leschetizky	Arabesque en forme d'Étude Op. 45, No. 1	54
Liszt	Hungarian Rhapsody No. 6	30
Mendelssohn	Prelude and Fugue in E Minor Op. 35, No. 1	64
	Rondo Capriccioso Op. 14	14
Moszkowski	Caprice Espagnol Op. 37	80
Paganini-Liszt	Campanella, La	147
Prokofieff	Gavotte Op. 12, No. 2	94
Rachmaninoff	Prélude in G Minor Op. 23, No. 5	48
Ravel	Jeux d'Eau	119
Schubert-Tausig	Marche Militaire	132
Schumann	Soaring Op. 12, No. 2	107
Scriabin	Étude Op. 2, No. 1	12
Shostakovich	Polka (L'Age d'or) Op. 22	26

Rhapsodie
(E♭ Major)

Revised and Edited by Maxwell Eckstein

JOHANNES BRAHMS, Op. 119, No. 4
(1833-1897)

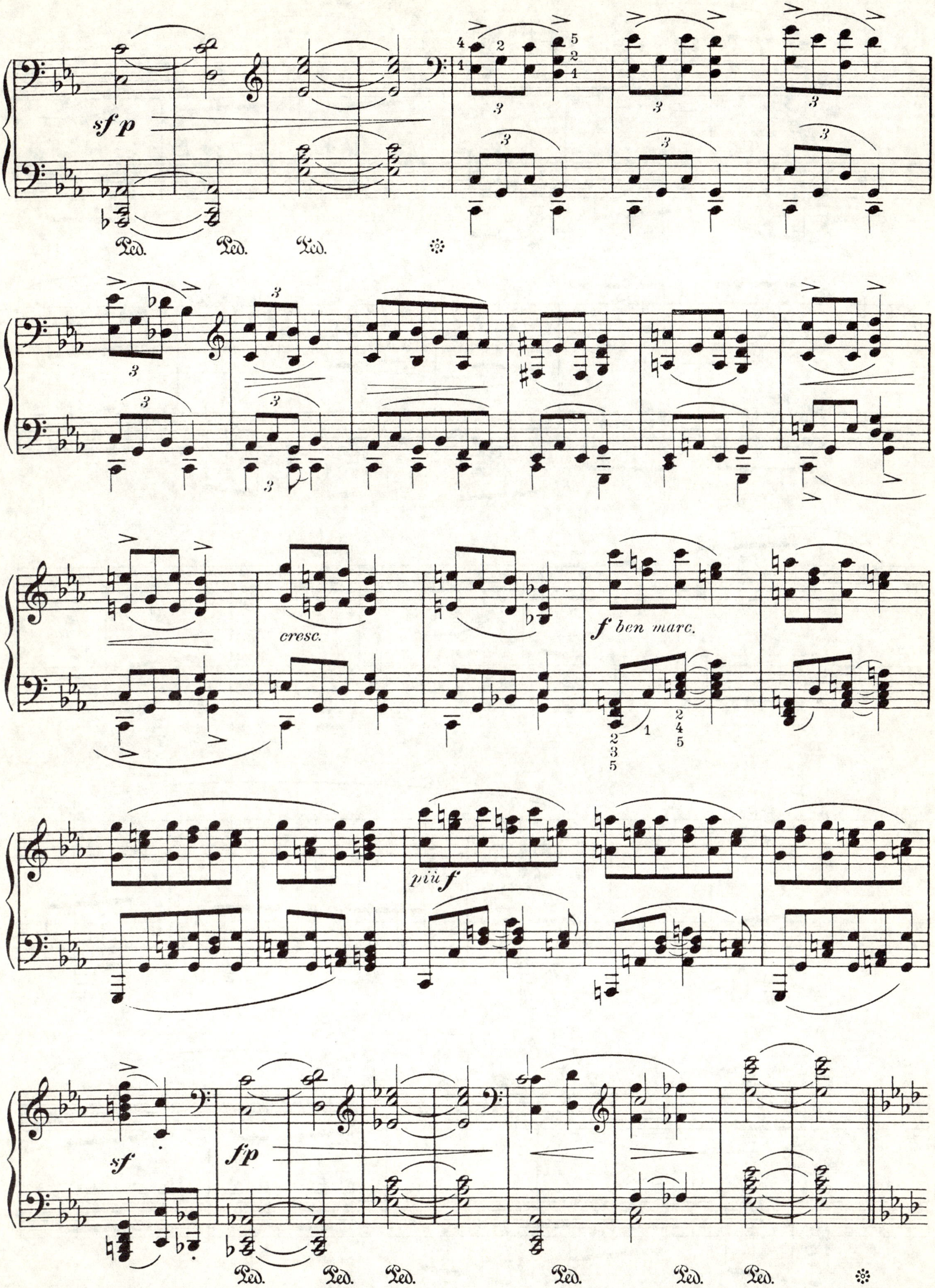
sf p
Ped.
Ped.
Ped.
cresc.
f ben marc.
più f
sf
fp
Ped.
Ped.
Ped.
Ped.
Ped.
Ped.

Étude

A. SCRIABIN, Op. 2, No. 1
(1872-1915)

Rondo Capriccioso

Revised and Edited by MAXWELL ECKSTEIN

F. MENDELSSOHN, Op. 14
(1809 – 1847)

Andante (♩ = 60)

* At this point there is a tendency to hurry. Do not increase the speed.

Copyright 1938 by Carl Fischer, Inc., New York

* The Presto to be played with a crisp touch.

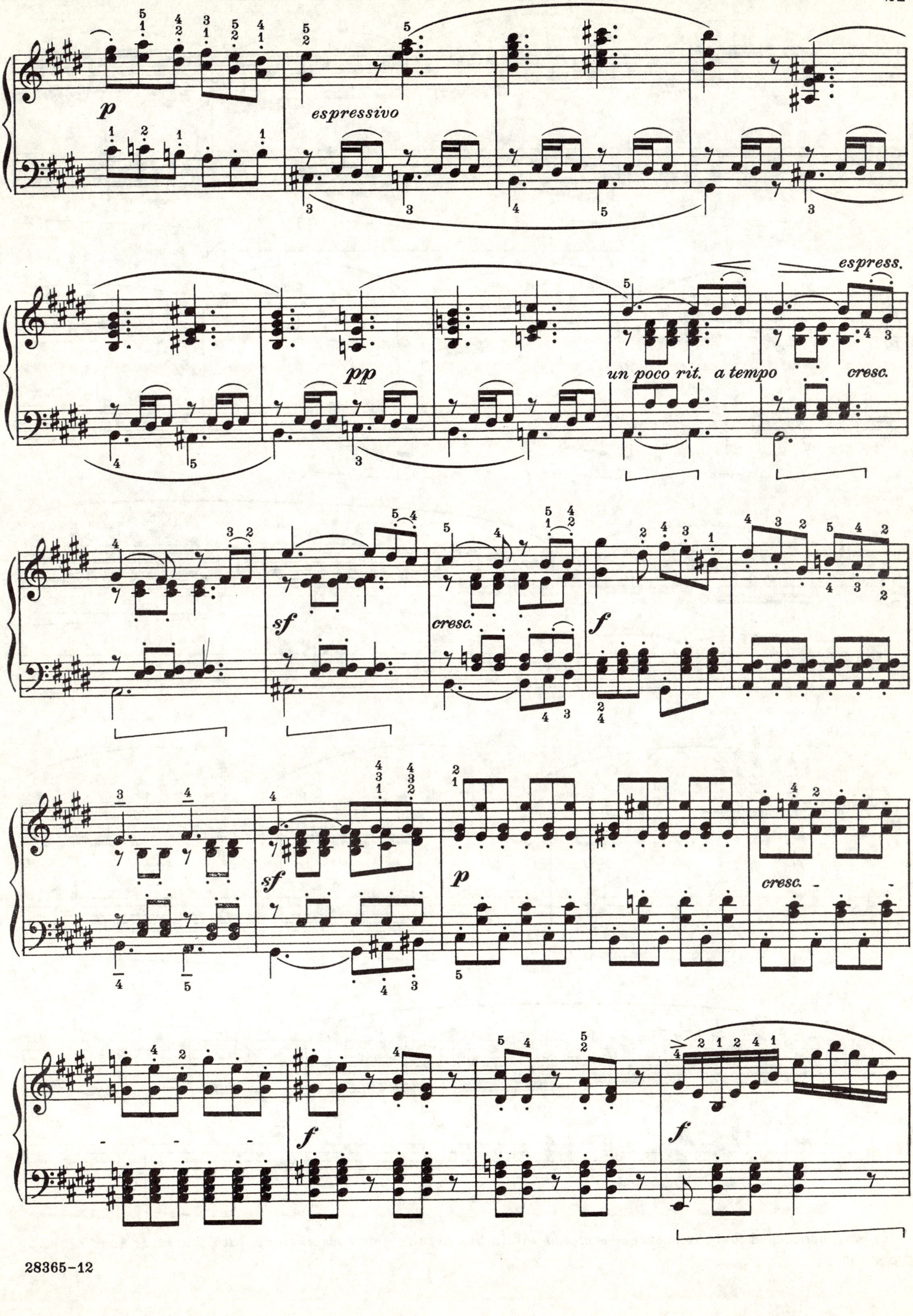
p
espressivo
pp
un poco rit.
a tempo
espress.
cresc.
sf
cresc.
f
sf
p
cresc.
f
f

* It is recommended that the passages enclosed within brackets receive *special study* with the *right hand alone*.

*See preceding note.

* Rhythmical accuracy is of extreme importance in this closing section.

Polka
from the Ballet "L'Age d'or"

D. SHOSTAKOVICH, Op. 22
Edited, revised and corrected
by Maxwell Eckstein

c) See a) preceding page

e) This A may be omitted

41

Seguidilla
Castilian Dance

Revised and Edited by Maxwell Eckstein

I. ALBENIZ (1860-1909)

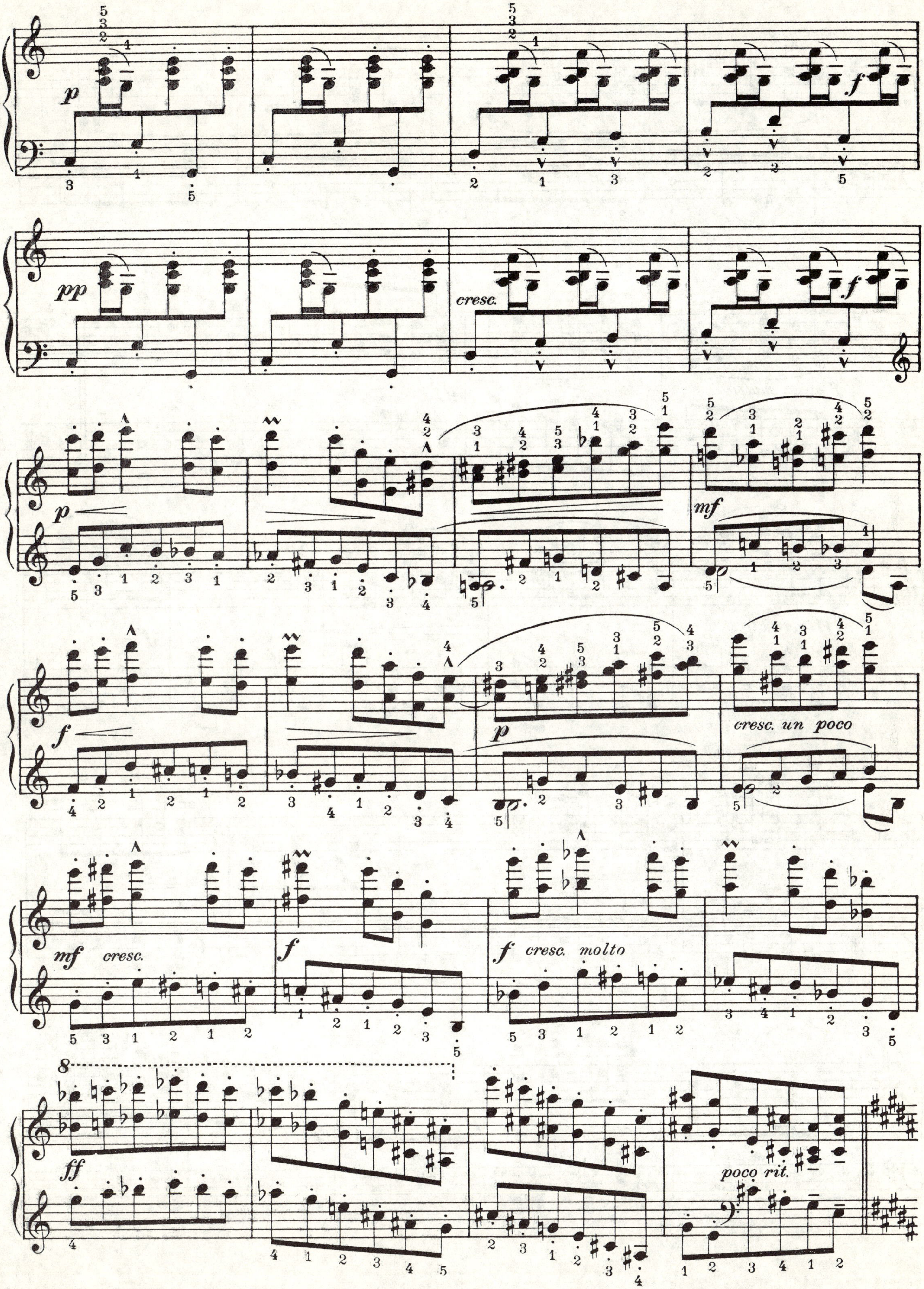
p
f
pp
cresc.
f
p
mf
f
p
cresc. un poco
mf cresc.
f
f cresc. molto
8
ff
poco rit.

Prélude

in G minor

Revised and Edited by Maxwell Eckstein

Sergei Rachmaninoff, Op. 23, Nº 5
(1873 - 1943)

Copyright 1943 by Carl Fischer, Inc., New York

Un poco meno mosso

Arabesque en forme d'Étude

Revised and Edited by Maxwell Eckstein

THEODOR LESCHETIZKY
(1830-1915)
Op. 45, No. 1

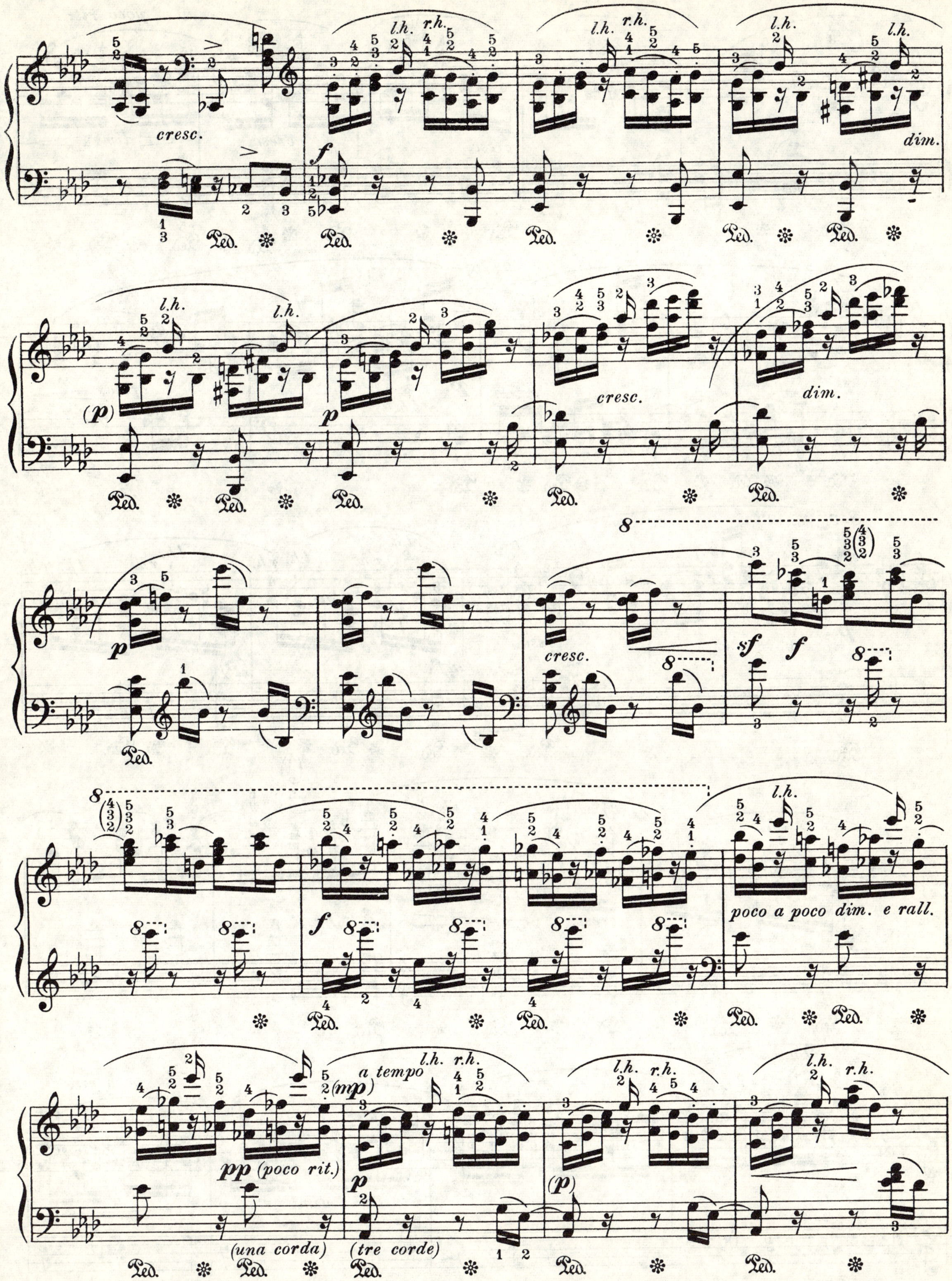
cresc.
dim.
l.h.
r.h.
Ped.
(p)
p
f
sf
poco a poco dim. e rall.
pp (poco rit.)
a tempo
(mp)
(una corda)
(tre corde)

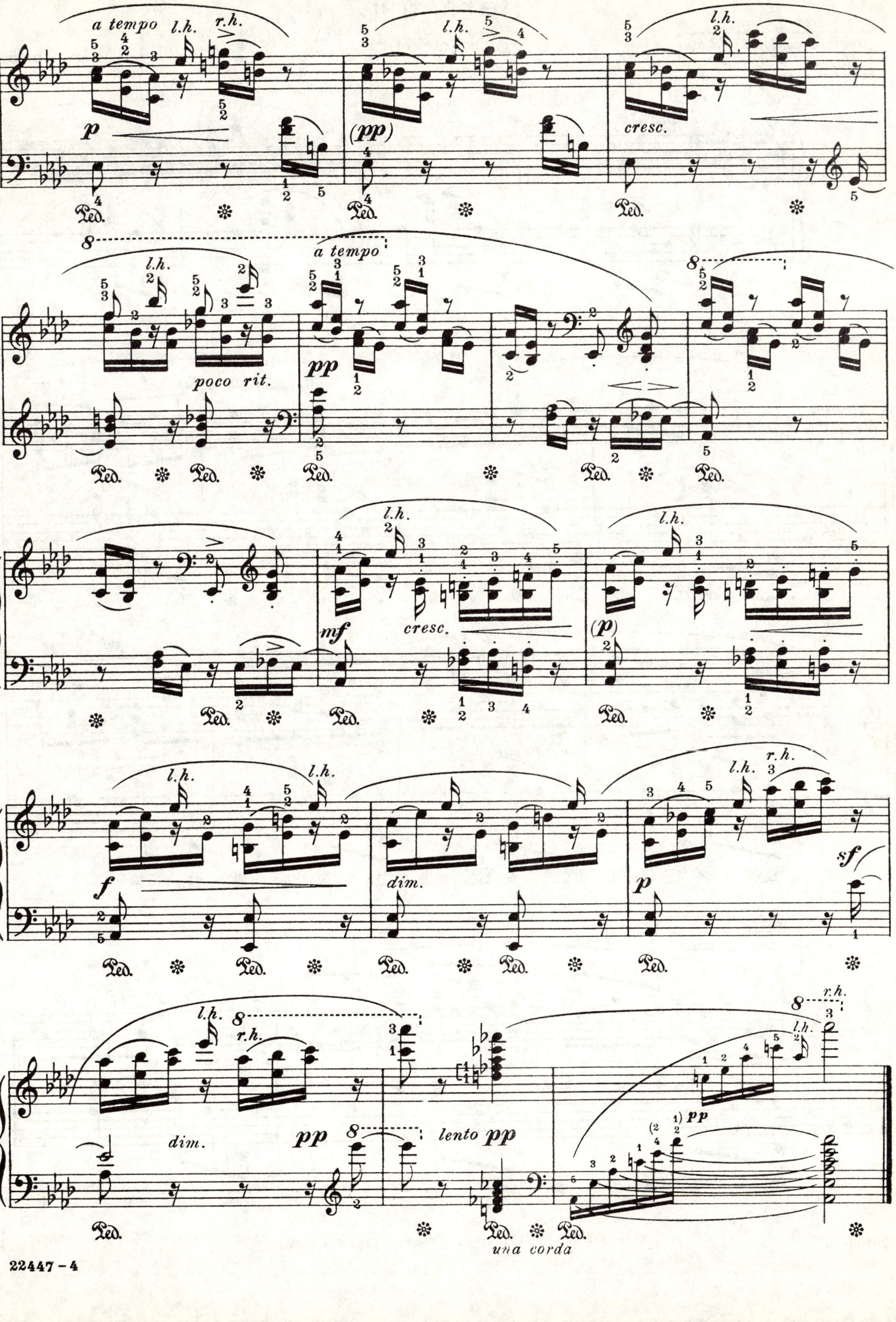
a tempo
l.h.
r.h.
p
(pp)
cresc.
poco rit.
pp
mf
(p)
f
dim.
sf
lento pp
una corda
Ped.

Berceuse
(Cradle Song)

FR. CHOPIN, Op. 57
(1810-1849)

Revised and Edited by Maxwell Eckstein

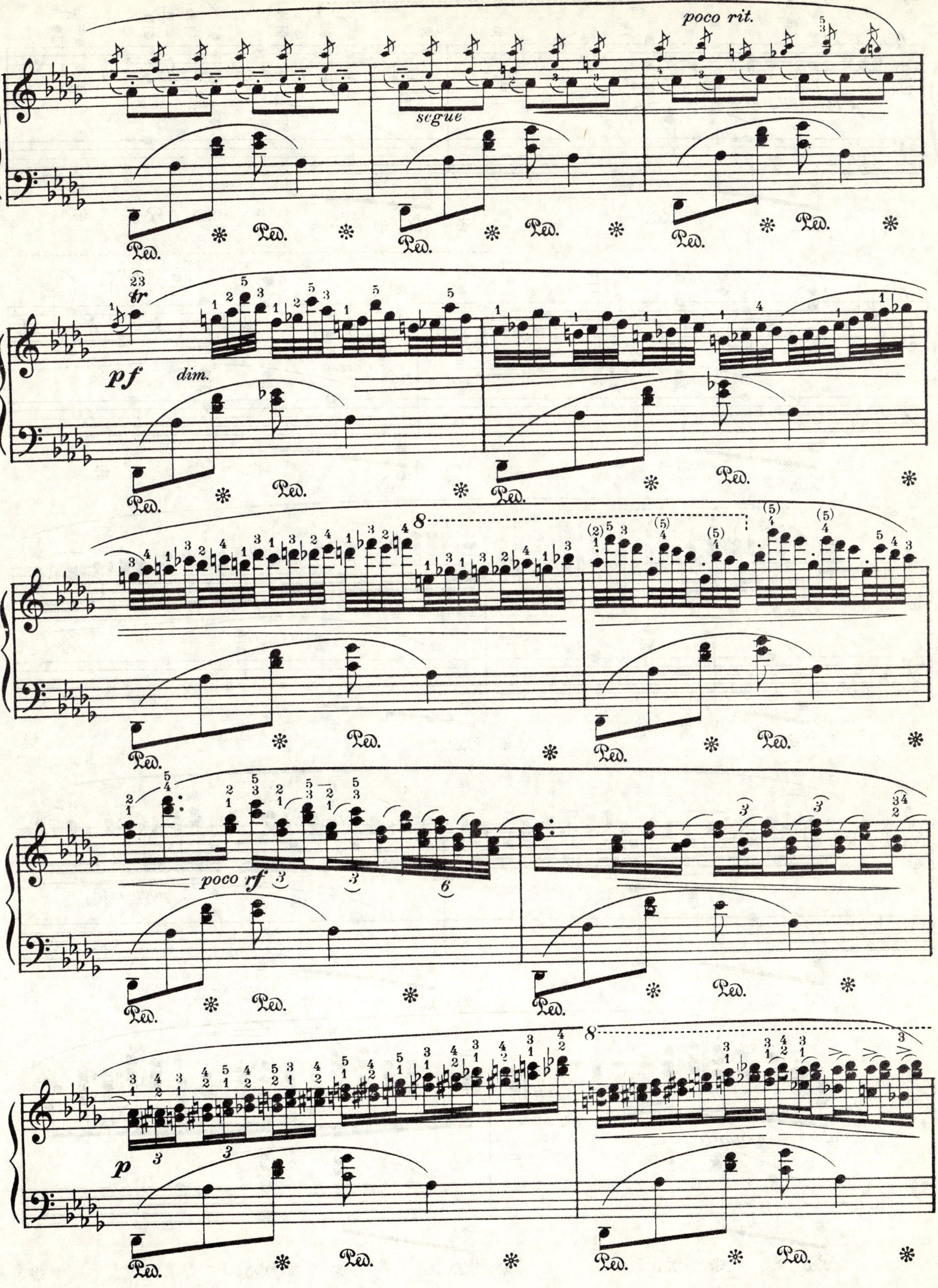
poco rit.
segue
pf
dim.
poco rf
p
Ped.

Prelude and Fugue in E Minor
(Composed in 1837)

Revised and Edited by Maxwell Eckstein

Prelude

F. Mendelssohn Bartholdy, Op. 35, No. 1
(1809 – 1847)

Fugue

71

Étude
(Butterfly)

F. CHOPIN, Op 25, No. 9
(1810–1849)

Revised and Edited by Maxwell Eckstein

Assai allegro (♩= 112)

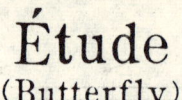

Caprice Espagnol

Revised and Edited by Maxwell Eckstein

Maurice Moszkowski, Op. 37
(1854-1925)

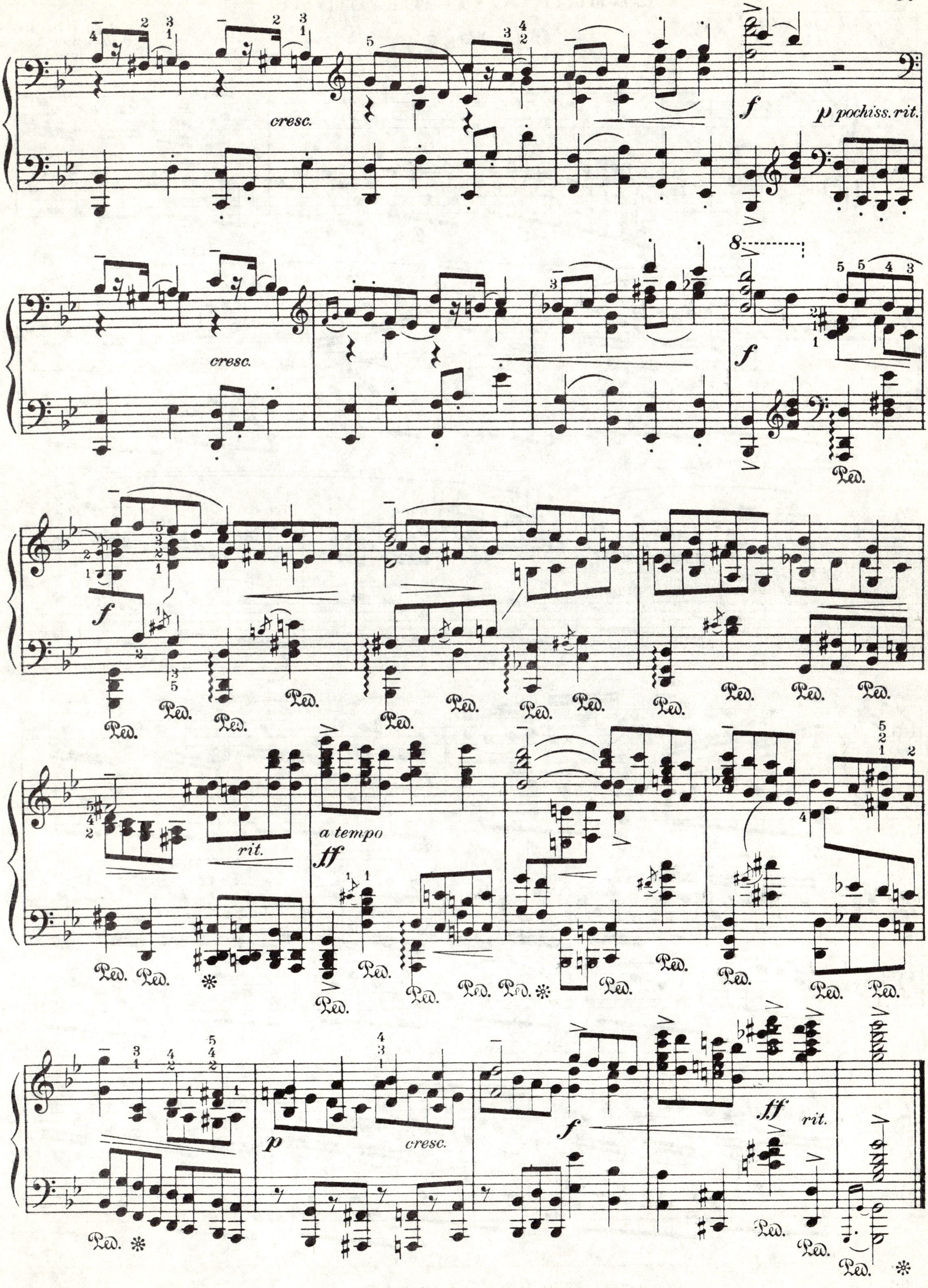
cresc.
f
p pochiss. rit.
cresc.
f
f
rit.
a tempo
ff
p
cresc.
f
ff
rit.

Fantaisie - Impromptu

in C sharp minor

Revised and Edited by Maxwell Eckstein

Fr. Chopin, Op. 66
(1810-1849)
(Posthumous)

Allegro agitato (𝅗𝅥 = 88)

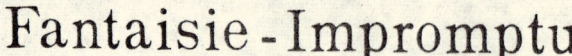

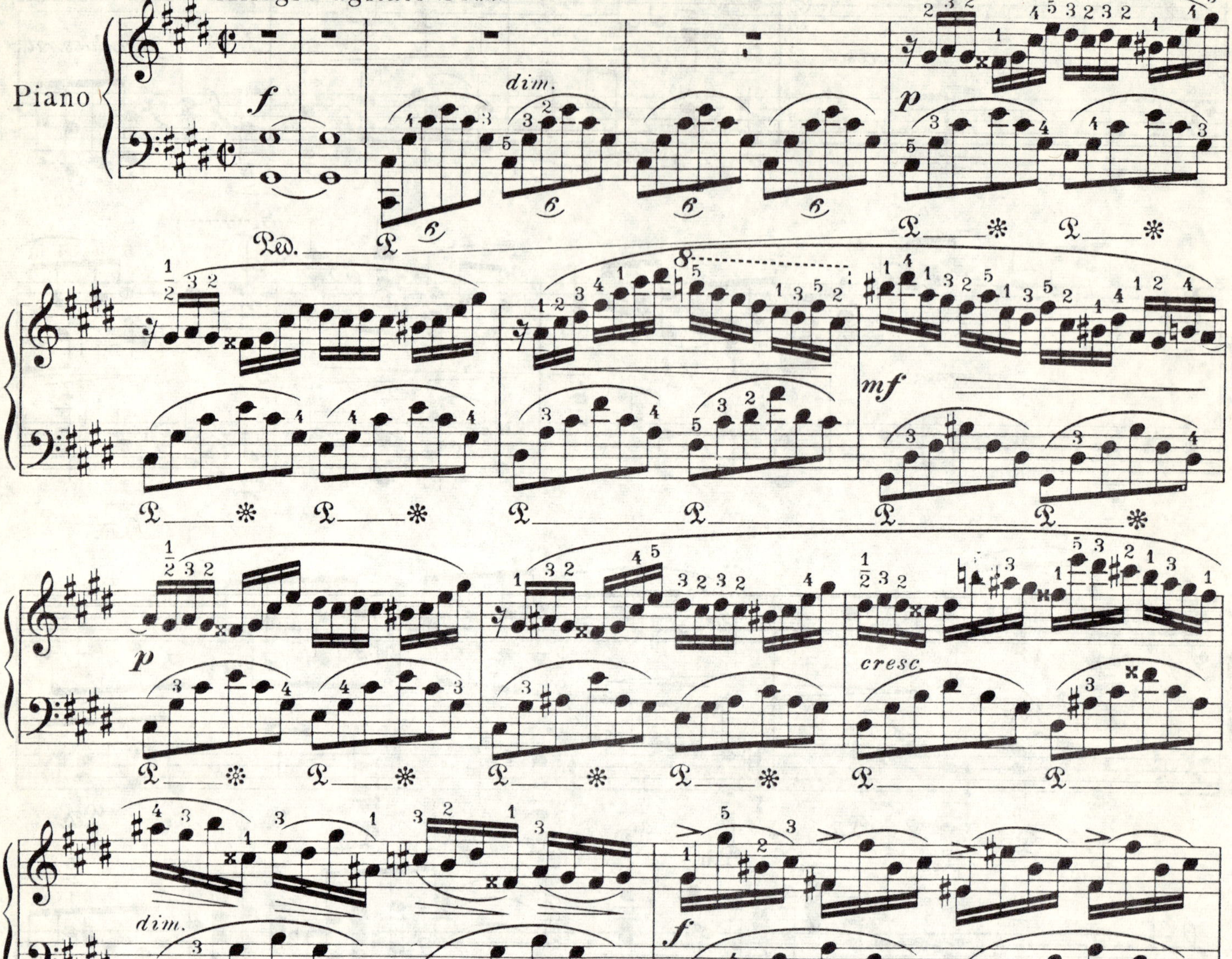

Soaring
(Aufschwung)

a) Divide this chord passage as follows: The notes with stems downward to be played with the left hand.

b) Same execution as under a) The octave in the bass however has to be left immediately after striking it and its continuation must be effected by means of the damper pedal.

Copyright MCMXLVIII by Carl Fischer, Inc., New York

108 *Con espressione*

a) See previous notes a) and b)

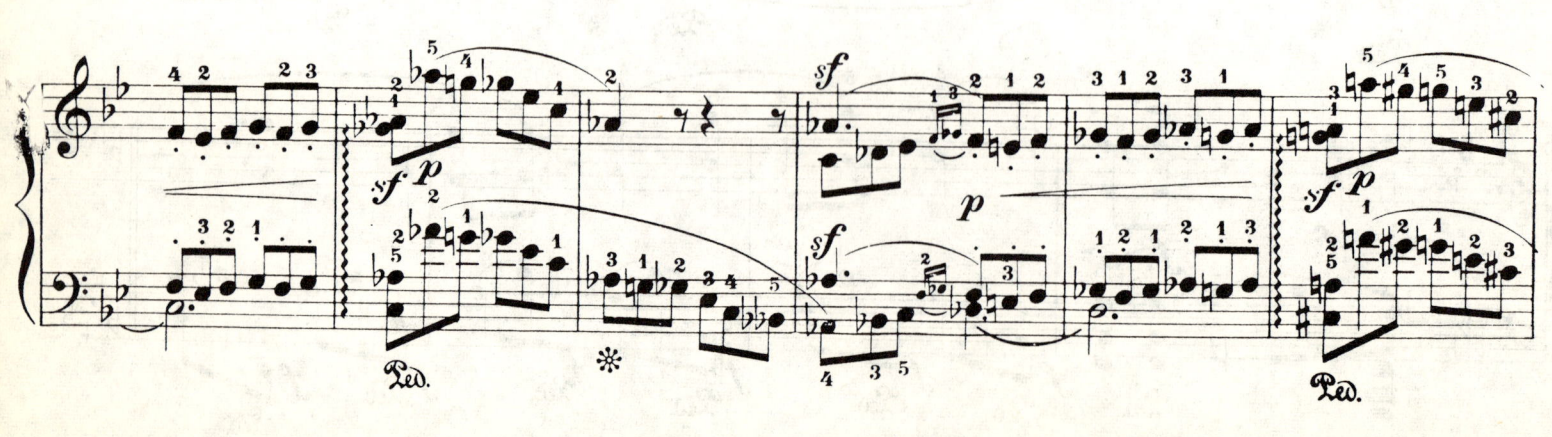

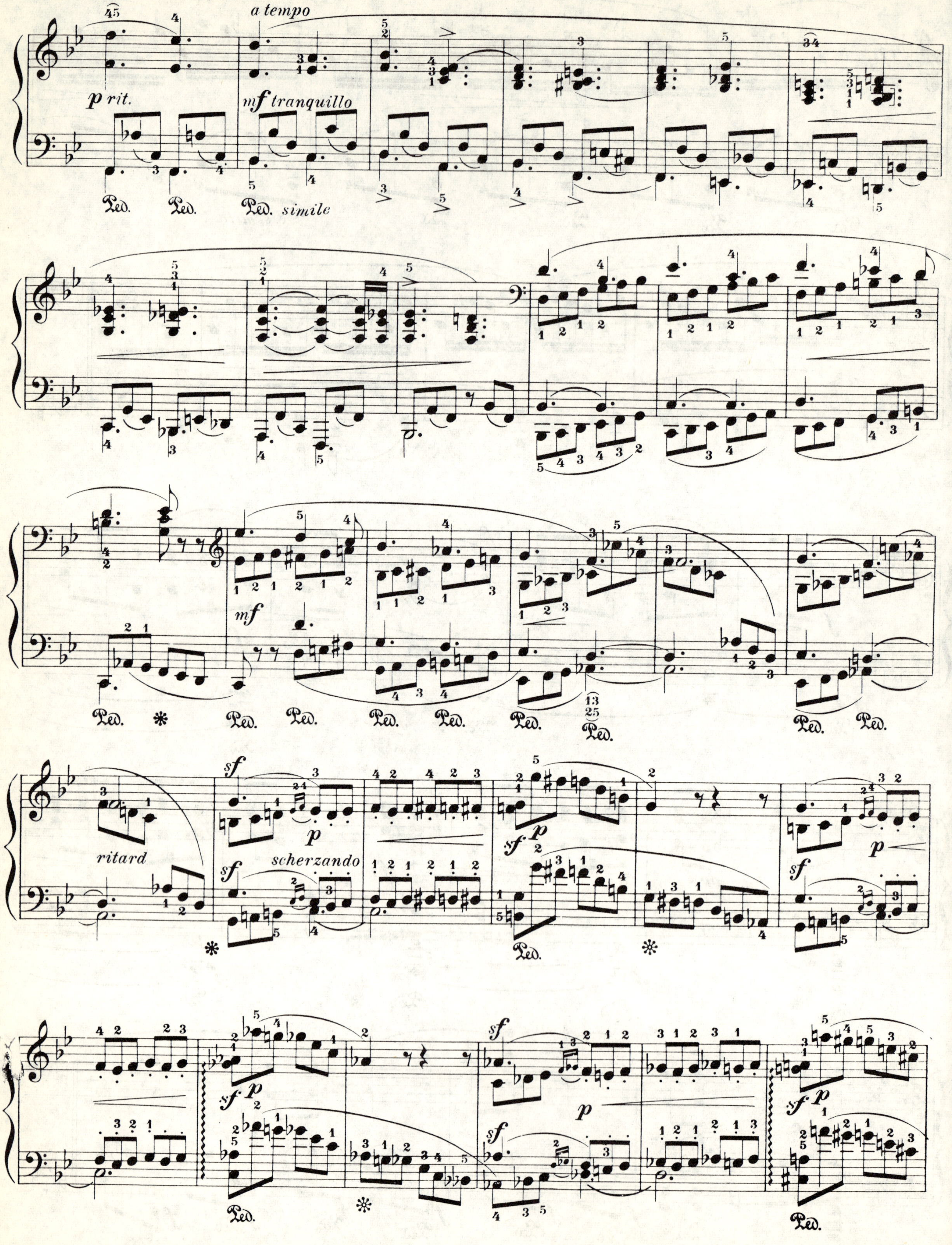
p rit.
a tempo
mf tranquillo
Ped. simile
ritard
sf
scherzando
mf

111

a) For small hands: [musical example] etc.

Étude
(Revolutionary)

Revised and Edited by Maxwell Eckstein

F. CHOPIN, Op. 10, No. 12
(1810-1849)

Allegro con fuoco (♩= 160)

29637   Copyright MCMXLVIII by Carl Fischer, Inc., New York

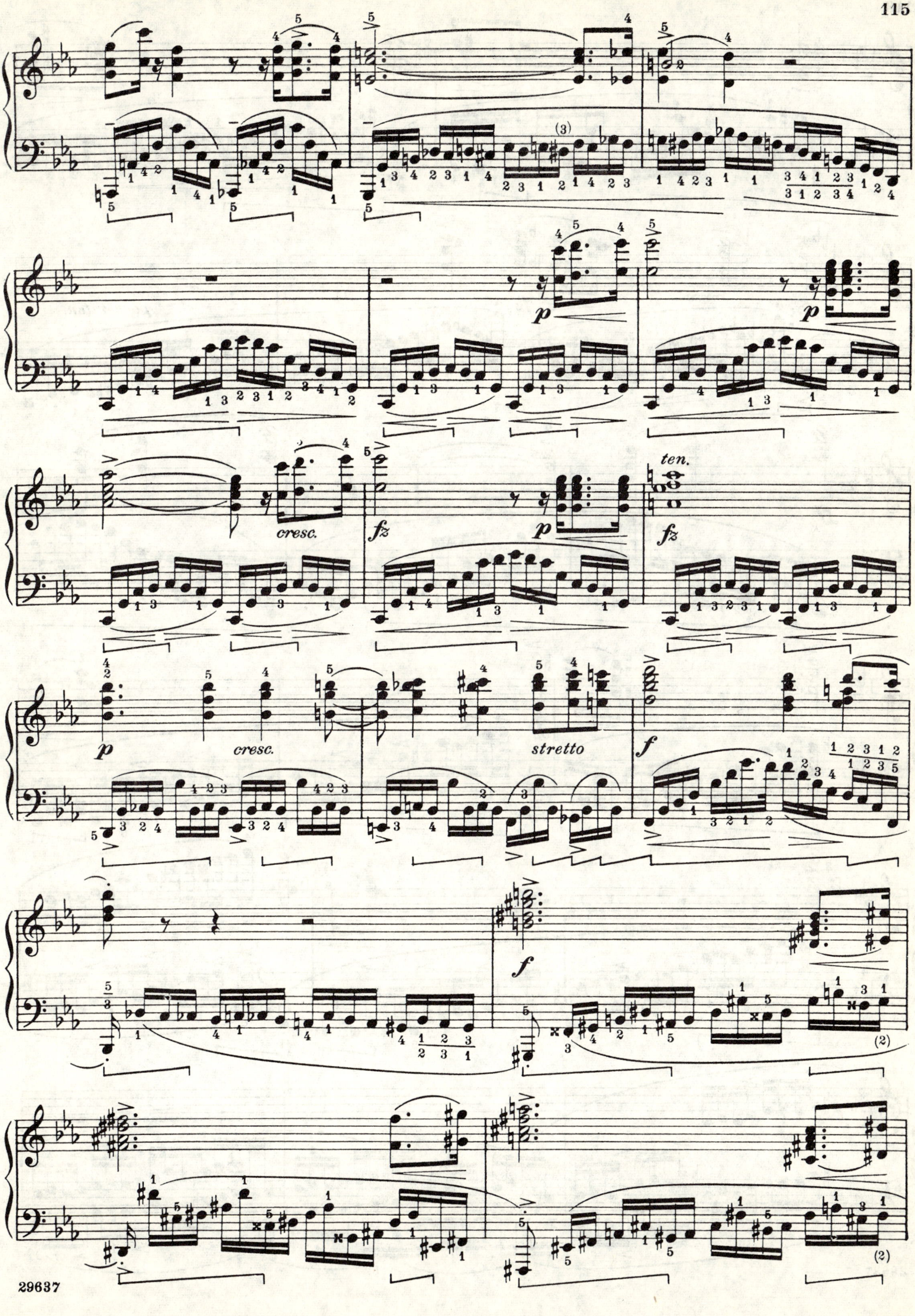
p
p
cresc.
fz
p
ten.
fz
p
cresc.
stretto
f
f

118

à mon cher Maître Gabriel Fauré

Jeux d'Eau

Dieu fluvial riant de l'eau qui le chatouille.
Henri de Régnier

MAURICE RAVEL
(1875-1937)

Revised and Edited by
Maxwell Eckstein

Copyright MCMXLVIII by Carl Fischer, Inc., New York

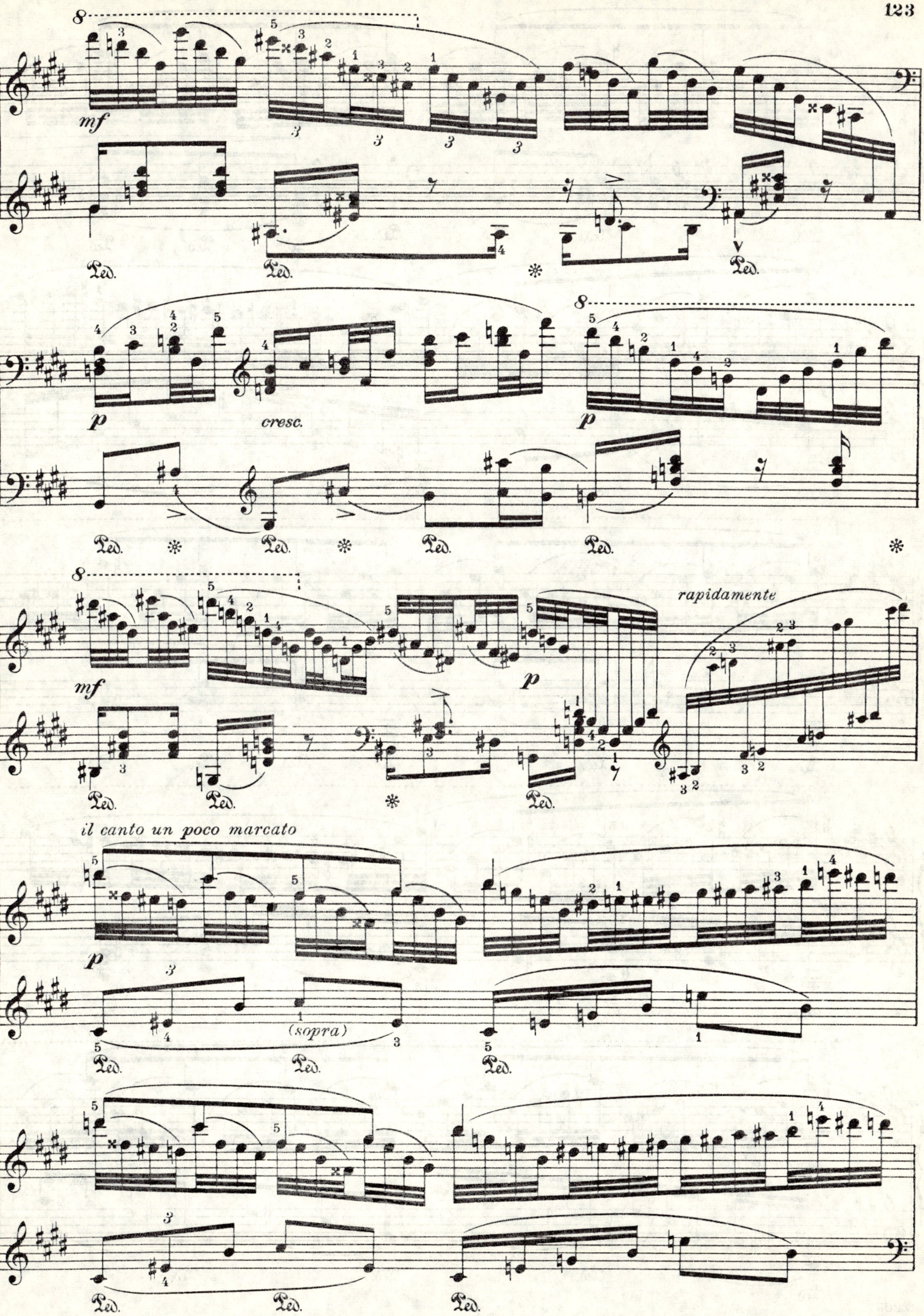
mf
p
cresc.
rapidamente
il canto un poco marcato
(sopra)

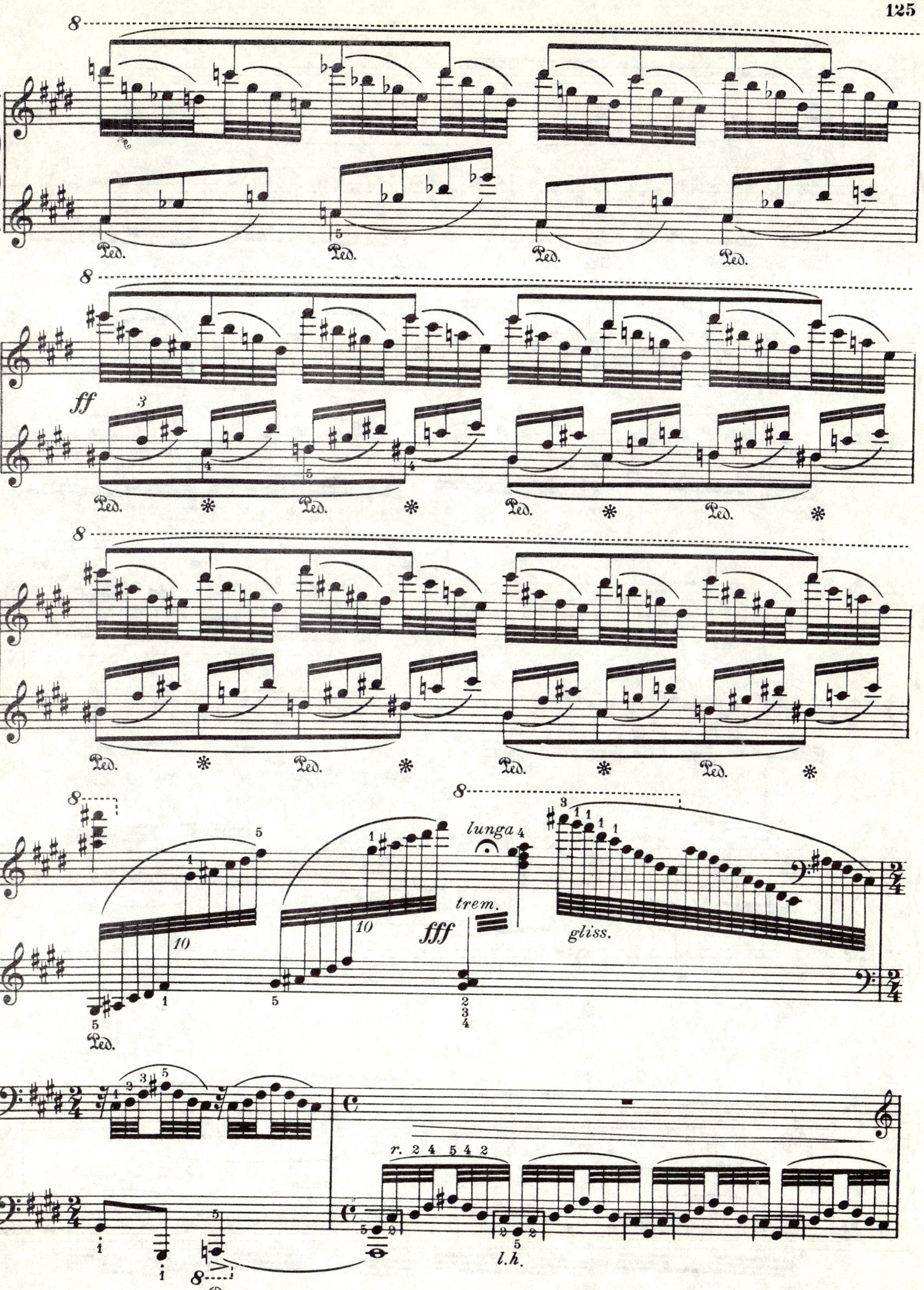
ff
lunga
trem.
fff
gliss.
l.h.
Ped.

131

Dedicated to Dr. Hans von Bülow

Marche Militaire

by
FRANZ SCHUBERT
Op. 51, No. 1

Revised and Edited by Maxwell Eckstein

Piano arrangement in concert-style by
CARL TAUSIG
(1841-1871)

Copyright MCMXLVI by Carl Fischer, Inc., New York

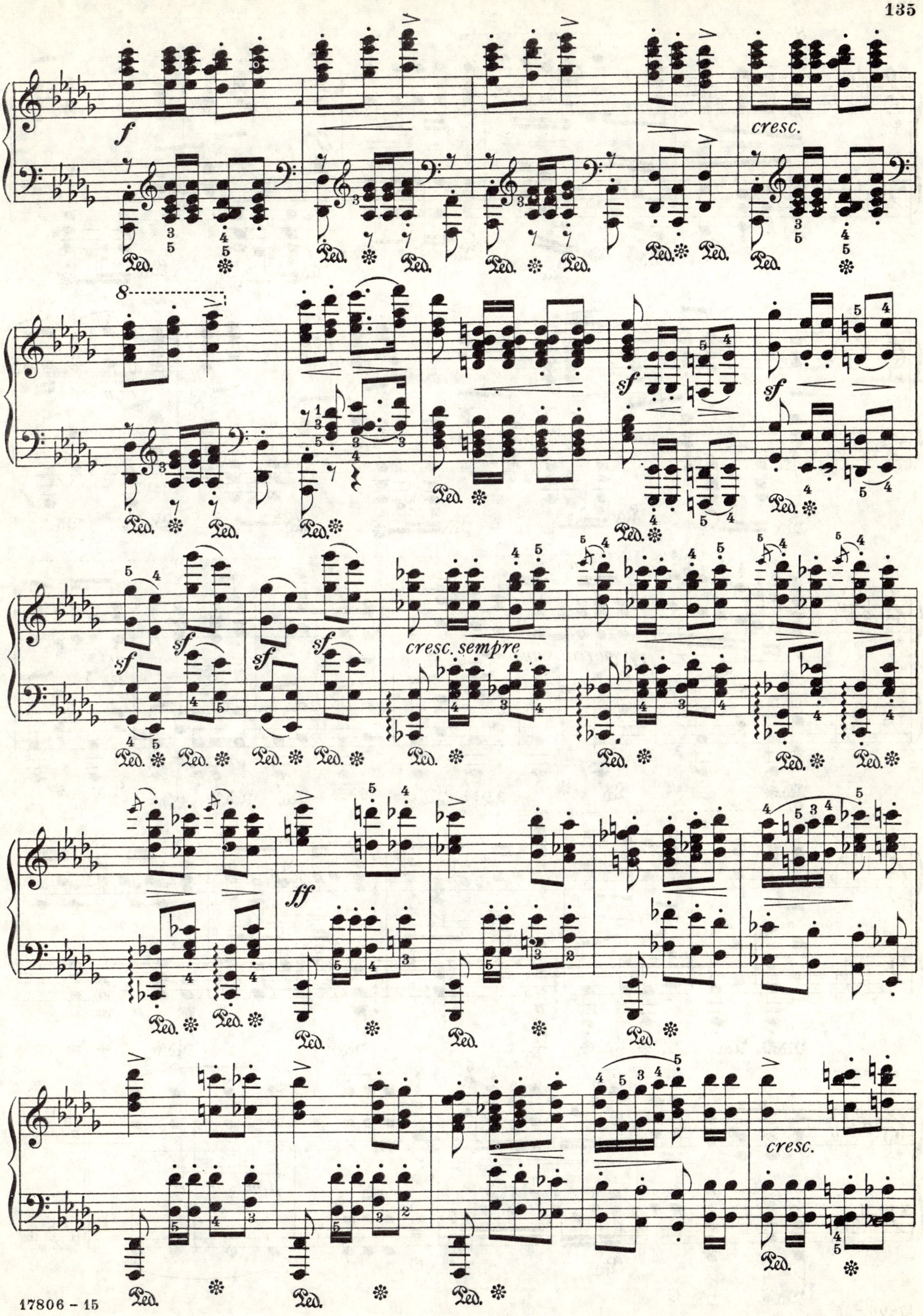
f
cresc.
Ped.
8
sf
cresc. sempre
ff
cresc.

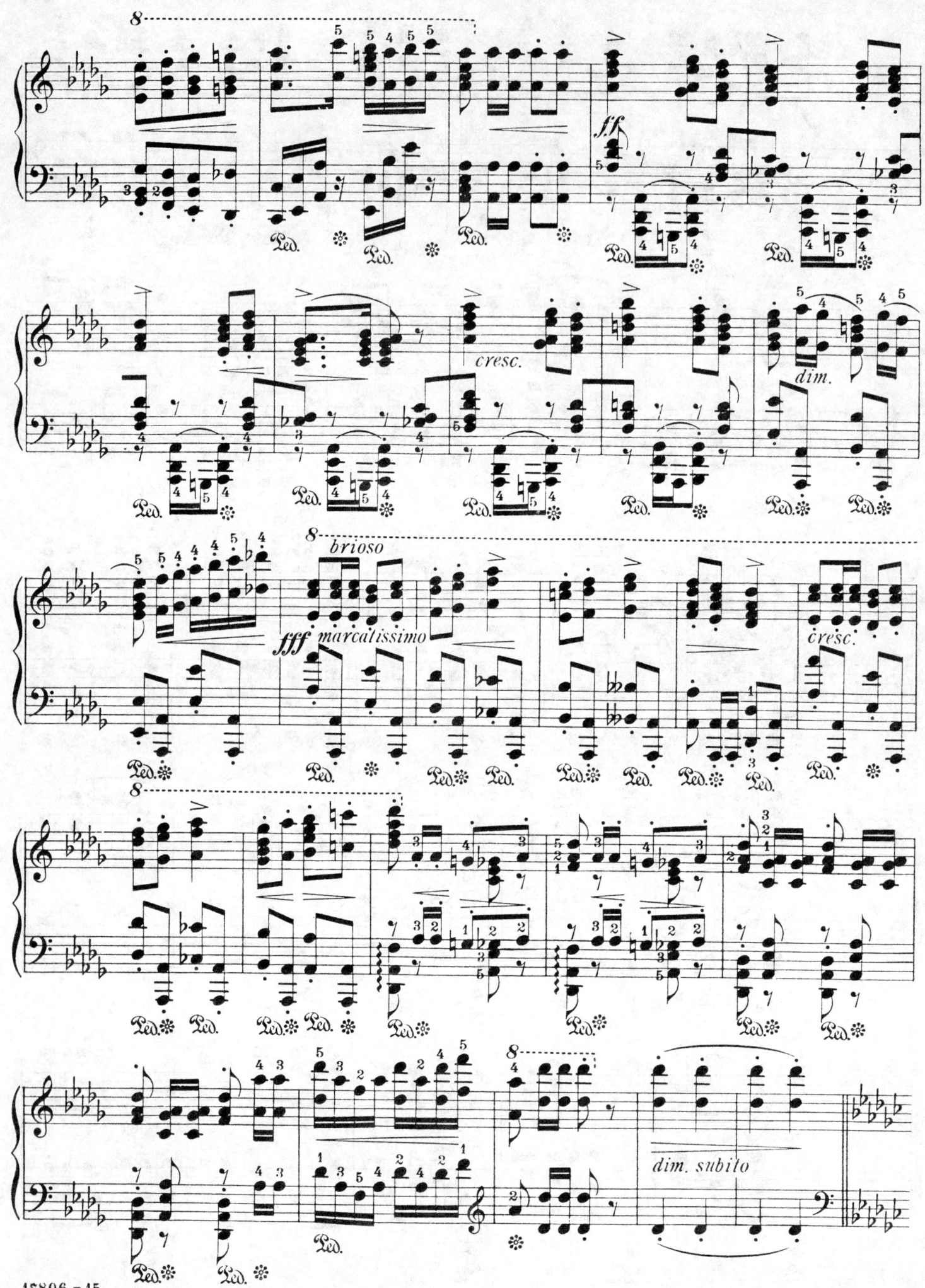

TRIO
Un poco più tranquillo ($\quarter = 92$)

140

La Campanella

by
N. PAGANINI

Revised and Edited by
Maxwell Eckstein

ETUDE de CONCERT

Transcribed by
FRANZ LISZT
(1811–1886)

Copyright MCMXLVI by Carl Fischer, Inc., New York

150

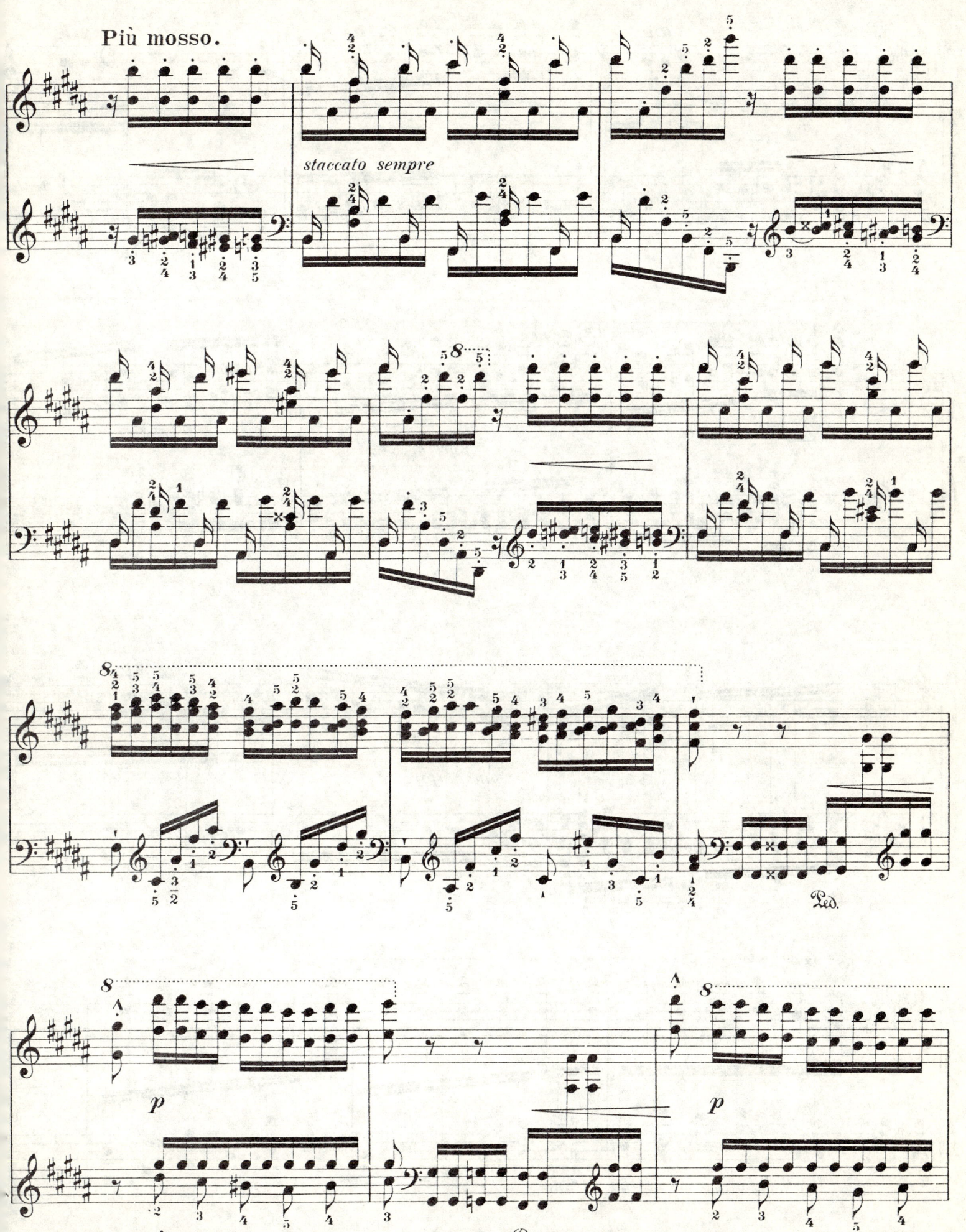